Be
SET FREE
From

Shame, Guilt
and
Condemnation

Be
SET FREE
From

Shame, Guilt
and
Condemnation

By Victor and Judy Chatellier

Be SET FREE From
Shame, Guilt and Condemnation

What people are saying:

"Being bound up by shame for most of my life I had read many books on the subject and all of them serve to only outline the problem but none of them showed a way out. I desperately wanted and needed to be set free from the constant deep sense of wrongness that had followed me around my entire life. I'm pleased to say I did find a way to be set free and his name is Jesus. You hold in your hand a map to follow to get you out of the darkness of shame and into the light of freedom from shame, guilt and condemnation."

- Judy C.

"The days of feeling trapped without a way of escape are over. I am extremely grateful for having found the way out of pain, deception, insecurity and finding realignment into harmony with my Creator and myself. Any person that is walking over this Earth will benefit from taking a walk thru Shame University. Fear not, only believe, freedom is here."

-Nancy M.

"There are gems of knowledge from God in this book that still affect how I see myself in the Spirit ever since I read it about six years ago. I hope a lot of people get to read this because as they do Jesus will lift weight off their shoulders that has been there for their whole life."

- Fienn M., Lieutenant USN

"Taught me compassion for others and myself."

- Nora R.

"This book and the accompanying audio book were incredibly eye opening for me. Not only did this book help me, but over the years I've also seen this book help many others. I believe shame, guilt and condemnation affect almost everyone. They're like an anchor keeping people stuck where they really don't want to be. This book shows how we can finally break free from that anchor."

-Chad Taylor

"Shame, guilt and condemnation are the roots of the pain no one talks about. In this book you will learn to uproot these problems and explore the only remedy for true healing."

- Nancy H.

**Scan this QR code to
listen to part one.
Or visit *thevoiceoftruth.net***

Part One

The old has passed away...

"Therefore, if anyone is in Christ, he is a new creation.
The old has passed away; behold, the new has come."

- 2 Corinthians 5:17 (ESV)

Most adults have a working knowledge of guilt and condemnation, so my focus will primarily be on shame because very few people have any concept at all of what shame is and how it affects our lives. Yet I've found shame to be very widespread and I'm astonished at the destruction it causes. God's people are destroyed by their lack of knowledge and I believe this message will equip us to destroy the works of the devil by victoriously waging war on shame.

The dictionary defines shame as:

1. A painful emotion caused by a strong sense of guilt, embarrassment, unworthiness, or disgrace.

2. Capacity for such a feeling: Have you no shame?

3. One that brings dishonor, disgrace, or condemnation.

4. A condition of disgrace or dishonor; ignominy.

5. A great disappointment.

6. To cause to feel shame; put to shame.

7. To bring dishonor or disgrace on

8. To force by making ashamed: He was shamed into making an apology.

9. To fill with shame; disgrace (my definition of dis-grace is distant from grace).

Let me give you my perception of the word shame as it pertains to this study. Shame is the *sense of wrongness* of the inner self. You believe your whole life is a mistake. You don't just think you did something wrong, you think your very existence is wrong. Like you shouldn't even be here, you don't belong here, or anywhere. You're just WRONG. You live your life on the verge of being overwhelmed by your inner sense of wrongness, and then you actually say or do something WRONG. Horror upon horror! First you just felt wrong, but now you really did something wrong thereby apparently proving that your feelings about yourself are true! Now you have outward evidence that *seems* to confirm your inner sense of wrongness. The thing you did wrong becomes the proverbial last straw that broke the camels back! So you totally overreact to the error and everybody looks at you like, *"What's "WRONG" with you"*?! And *that* is the absolute last question you ever wanted anybody to ask about you and now everybody is asking it! Shame heaped upon shame.

The *fear* of this scenario causes you to lock up and you progressively disengage and withdraw from people who get close to you to avoid the fearful possibility of your carefully hidden shame being found out. People in shame think, "I want to do it so right but I'm afraid to do it wrong so I get stuck in between and I can't move from my position. I'm held captive by my fear of *wrong*. I'm so ashamed that I can't bear even one more instance of being *wrong*."

Rather than endure the terrible torment of being lonely, the victims of shame invent social "masks" of wrongness and rightness to disguise and cover their shameful inner sense of wrongness. Some people develop a wrongness mask where they are able to hide in full view of everybody. It's called worm theology and it says to whoever will listen, "I'm a total low life loser" or some similar version of frequent negative statements about themselves. They develop a morbid fondness for self denunciation and they actually become more comfortable in being wrong than in being right. I'll talk more about the wrongness mask later in this message but at this point let me move on to the rightness mask.

This mask presents an outer appearance of right speaking and right doing. They work so hard on their rightness mask that they become the dreaded "perfectionist." They spend huge amounts of energy to create the illusion of the perfect life.

Life is not perfect and we are not perfect. We are not even good. We're not even okay. We are all sinners saved by God's grace. The only time any of us are ever good, or right or perfect is when our spirit disappears in the Holy Spirit. I'm going to say it as simply as I can; if you walk in the flesh, you're wrong. If you walk in the Spirit, you're right. I'll come back to that statement in a moment but first let me say that guilt and condemnation are often the result, the fruit, the conscious and or unconscious evidence, confirming a deep inner belief system based on the grave clothes of wrongness, the burial shroud of shame. The longer a person stays in shame, the more numb or deadened they feel inside. I'll illustrate with a scriptural metaphor.

"When Jesus had said this, He shouted with a loud voice, Lazarus, come out! And out walked the man who had been dead, his hands and feet wrapped in burial cloths (linen strips), and with a [burial] napkin bound around his face. Jesus said to them, Free him of the burial wrappings and let him go."

- John 11:43-44

The NIV reads, *"Take off the grave clothes and let him go."* As the Holy Spirit began to teach me about shame He used the metaphor of grave clothes or burial cloths to give me a "word picture" so I could understand how shame works and where it resides in us.

However, before I get into the when, where and how of shame, let me say something far more important. Jesus loves *you*. Jesus promised to never leave you or forsake *you*. Jesus is very compassionate and He knows what is going on inside of *you*. He knows *you*. He feels what you feel and it moves Him to tears.

"When Jesus saw her sobbing, and the Jews who came with her [also] sobbing, He was deeply moved in spirit and troubled. [He chafed in spirit and sighed and was disturbed.] And He said, Where have you laid him? They said to Him, Lord, come and see. Jesus wept. The Jews said, See how [tenderly] He loved him!"

- John 11:33-36

I say see how tenderly He loves you. He wants to take the grave clothes of shame, guilt and condemnation off of you and *"let you go"* so you can live life and that more abundantly. Jesus frees people and lets them go, with His words, the same way He does everything.

For the rest of this message I will purpose to let *His* words flow from my mouth, to your heart and soul. Please purpose to hear. I believe that shame is the grave clothes, the mummification, the en-capsulation of your spirit. **Hebrews 4:12** tells us there is a dividing line between soul and spirit and that is the dwelling place of shame. That's why you may have at times felt a disconnect between your spirit and your soul. When I say spirit I'm speaking of your heart and when I say soul I'm speaking of your mind, will and emotions. Shame resides in the line between spirit and soul and hinders the flow between the two. Small shame creates small hindrance and great shame creates severe disconnect.

Not only are your closest people unable to touch your heart but you yourself are out of touch with your innermost feelings and thoughts. Numb inside like you're not even there. A mummy is a good metaphor. You're walking around like you're alive, but inside you're numb, as though you were dead. People don't understand you and you don't understand them. There's no connection. You can be alone in a crowded room full people that know your name, but they don't know you. You don't even know you, but there is One Who does know you. His Name is Jesus and you need only follow the sound of His voice and He will lead you right out of this dark cave and then He will command, *"Take off the grave clothes and let him go."*

You might have wondered just now, *"How will I hear His voice"*? If you are stirred by what you have been hearing right now, then you already know and hear His voice. Scripture teaches that His voice, His word and His Truth are all One. If you are not moved inside by what you're hearing right now then I ask you to keep on listening because He will keep on calling out to you.

"He shouted with a loud voice, Lazarus, come out!" He will never give up on you and He needs only the smallest cooperation from you to do miraculous things in your life. We need only do the easy part like *"roll the stone away to open the tomb"* and then He will do the hard part like bring life out of death and then glory out of shame. He may not ask you to open a tomb but He is asking you right now to open your ears. You do that by making the decision that you expect to hear something good. **Hosea 2:15** says that God will open a door of hopeful expectation right in the place of your trouble. God wants to turn your bad into good.

> "Instead of your [former] shame you shall have a twofold recompense; instead of dishonor and reproach [your people] shall rejoice in their portion. Therefore in their land they shall possess double [what they had forfeited]; everlasting joy shall be theirs."
>
> - Isaiah 61:7

Our part is to let Him, by believing what He says. It's called faith and He already gave you the sufficient measure of faith to believe what is being said to you right now. He is asking you not to oppose yourself by resisting or doubting what is being said right now. It's not all about you, it's all about Him. Please let Him help you by believing His words more than your own thoughts and feelings. One of mankind's most destructive enemies is the idolatry of SELF; the fake God called *"ME, MYSELF and I."*

1 John 3:20 speaks of our own hearts tormenting us with self-accusation and making ourselves feel guilty and condemned. That is an important verse and I'll come back to it later in this message but the point here is this; because we ourselves are our own adversary; we need someone else to save us, from us. *We* brought upon ourselves the problem of sin and death and Jesus solved our problem.

You'll hear that concept perfectly stated here:

"But *He* was wounded for *our* transgressions, *He* was bruised for *our* guilt and iniquities; the chastisement [needful to obtain] peace and well-being for *us* was upon *Him*, and with the stripes [that wounded] *Him* *we* are healed and made whole. All *we* like sheep have gone astray, *we* have turned every one to *his* own way; and the Lord has made to light upon *Him* the guilt and iniquity of *us* all."

- Isaiah 53:5-6

Notice there was no mention of the devil at all. God probably speaks a thousand times more about our choices than He does about the devils influence. The *"devil made me do it"* is just a thinly veiled attempt to blame someone else, for our choice. I'm sorry if this scuffs your well polished theology but just as we can do no good apart from Jesus, so also the devil can do no bad in our life without man's permission. Now you might say *"I didn't tell the devil yes"* and I would have to ask *"Did you tell him no?"*

Not choosing is itself, a choice. Not resisting the devil is, by default, submitting to him. If the devil cannot get our cooperation, he can still complete his mission using our apathy. In the garden Eve was cooperative and Adam was apathetic. He stood silently by and watched what was happening without resisting and exercising his God-given dominion and authority. Either way, the devil won that battle but he will certainly lose the war and his loss will come sooner as we take some responsibility for our choices.

After the fall, Adam blamed his wife and she blamed the serpent and they all got cursed. Listen to this church. Put your ears on and purpose to hear this statement; *Wherever there's blame, there's shame.* Blame comes from shame, and produces only more shame. I believe every single time you blame someone, you're working for the devil. You're spreading demonic seed all over the people you say you love. You might want to pause this message and confess sin right now. Here I'll lead you in prayer. Please repeat after me.

"Father forgive me, I didn't know what I was doing. I was blind but now I see. I blamed (now say the name of the person you blame most often) Say it. I blamed (say the name)_____ when I myself was not innocent. I cast the first stone of blame, and I confess that it was sinful to allow corrupt communication out of my mouth, and I know You are Faithful and Just, and You forgive my sin, and cleanse me of all wrongness, and I am at this moment, restored to rightness thanks to You, for I ask it in Jesus name. Amen."

Well done!

"He shall see [the fruit] of the travail of His soul and be satisfied; by His knowledge of Himself [which He possesses and imparts to others] shall My [uncompromisingly] righteous One, My Servant, justify many AND make many righteous (upright and in "right" standing with God), for He shall bear their iniquities and their guilt [with the consequences, says the Lord]."

- Isaiah 53:11

Who did God say would justify and make you righteous? God thinks He is the One that justifies and makes us righteous; Himself not yourself. In fact, the harder we try to be good, the worse it gets because unbeknownst to us; we're trying to be our own god. Any time we attempt to be good and do good in our own human power all we accomplish is to heap more guilt and shame upon ourselves.

"Then they sweep by like a wind and pass on, and they load themselves with guilt, [as do all men] whose own power is their god."

- Habakkuk 1:11

This is the theme of Romans Chapter seven. When I want to do right, it ends up wrong. When I want to do good it ends up bad. When will we finally learn the truth of **John 15:51** that *"apart from Him, we can do nothing"?* Without His help we are all lost.

"For the Lord God helps Me; "THEREFORE" have I not been ashamed or confounded. "THEREFORE" have I set My face like a flint, and I know that I shall not be put to shame."

- Isaiah 50:7

"I will make your forehead like the hardest stone, harder than flint. Do not be afraid of them or terrified by them, though they are a rebellious house."

- Ezekiel 3:9 (NIV)

"And set your minds and keep them set on what is above (the higher things), not on the things that are on the earth. 3 For [as far as this world is concerned] you have died, and your [new, real] life is hidden with Christ in God."

- Colossians 3:2-3

"For those who are according to the flesh and are controlled by its unholy desires set their minds on and pursue those things which gratify the flesh, but those who are according to the Spirit and are controlled by the desires of the Spirit "set their minds" on and seek those things which gratify the [Holy] Spirit."

- Romans 8:5

We can set our minds and KNOW that He has made us clean, He has called us out of our cave, He helps us remove the dirty old grave clothes but we can do none of these things ourselves.

"For though you *wash yourself* with lye and use much soap, yet your iniquity and guilt are still [upon you; you are] spotted, dirty, and stained before Me, says the Lord."

- Jeremiah 2:22

There will be no spot no blemish
when we trust and allow Him to wash us.

In **Isaiah 1:18** God says He wants us to *"reason together with Him"* and then, *"though our sins be as scarlet, they shall be as white as snow."* But we must reason with Him and not reason within ourselves.

In **Revelation 3:18** Jesus counsels us to *"purchase from Him white clothes to keep the shame of our nudity from being seen."* You purchase from Christ by accepting the trade on the cross. His life for yours and your life for His. The majority of church folks never quite get around to finalizing the trade. They stop along the Way and cling to some part of their lives, never realizing that the part of their life they attempt to hide from God is the exact same place where shame dwells. I hope you heard that. Sell out to Christ. Complete the trade. Close the escrow. I referred to **Revelation 3:18** a mome nt ago but now I want to read the full verse to you.

"Therefore I counsel you to purchase from Me gold refined and tested by fire, that you may be [truly] wealthy, and white clothes to clothe you and to keep the shame of your nudity from being seen, and salve to put on your eyes, that you may see."

- Revelation 3:18

Nudity here means being "exposed," being "found out." You've spent a lifetime in what you believe to be your shameful true identity, hiding your wrongness, but Jesus now counsels you to acquire, by faith, His white robes of rightness before God. God is asking you to trust Him to take care of your shame problem and if you say yes to Him, you begin immediately to come out of your shame pit and He begins to remove the dead shame identity from you and cover you with His beautiful rightness. However there is a danger here. If you refuse to let your trust rest on Him and you persist in continuing your vain futile, attempts to hide and cover up your shame, then one day your worst fears will come to pass because that which you have believed, will become your reality as Jesus taught in **Matthew 8:13**.

Once you have chosen to believe and trust Christ to cover you with His rightness clothes then you will have to abide, to stay, in Christ and stay scripturally alert to guard your new white clothes from lying thoughts in your mind. The way out of shame is to stay in Christ.

> "And now, little children, abide (live, remain permanently) in Him, so that when He is made visible, we may have and enjoy perfect confidence (boldness, assurance) and not be ashamed and shrink from Him at His coming."
>
> - 1 John 2:28

You are in Christ when you hear His word and then do what you heard. Live that way and stay scripturally alert.

In **Revelation 16:15** Jesus says, "Behold, I am going to come like a thief! Blessed (happy, to be envied) is he who stays awake (alert) and who "guards his clothes," so that he may not be naked and [have the shame of being] seen exposed!"

White clothes are a metaphor of rightness and can only come from Jesus and are purchased at the cost of coming out of your hiding cave and surrendering the grave clothes and your own fake self righteousness clothes. Strip off your grave clothes and put on Christ. Clothe yourself with Christ.

Romans 13:14 says to *"clothe yourself with the Lord Jesus Christ"* and we do that by disappearing in Him. In just the same way your body disappeared for a moment as you were fully immersed in water at your baptism, in that same manner your spirit, and then your soul disappear in Jesus as you immerse your words, thoughts, deeds, motives and plans into His. Progressively be baptized, increasingly immersed, into Christ.

Listen to **Galatians 3:27**; "For as many [of you] as were baptized into Christ [into a spiritual union and communion with Christ, the Anointed One, the Messiah] have put on, (clothed yourselves, with) Christ."

As you decrease, He increases. People see less and less of you and more and more of Him.

Your reality progressively becomes **Galatians 2:20**; "I have been crucified with Christ [in Him I have shared His crucifixion]; it is no longer I who live, but Christ (the Messiah) lives in me; and the life I now live in the body I live by faith in (by adherence to and reliance on and complete trust in) the Son of God, Who loved me and gave Himself up for me."

There is no shame in Christ, so as His higher life increases, the lower, shame filled life decreases.

"Whoever finds his [lower] life will lose it [the higher life], and whoever loses his [lower] life on My account will find it [the higher life]."

- Matthew 10:39

Whatever you're seeking for in yourself and in others, that's what you will find. If you're always scanning for what's wrong, you will certainly find wrong. If you're scanning for what's right, you will surely find rightness, in yourself and others. I believe it is mandatory to find the righteousness of Christ in ourselves before we are able to find rightness in others.

You may ask, *"How fast can this transformation take place"*? How fast will you surrender your old lower life to Him? **Matthew 7:2** shows that your own measure will be used to measure back to you so I ask again, *"How fast will you surrender your old lower life to Him?"* That's how fast your transformation will take place. Don't act like you have forever to put on your white wedding clothes because none of us knows how long we have. Begin to strip off your old grave clothes and your own self righteousness hiding clothes now, while there's still time.

> "But when the king came in to meet the guests, he noticed a man who wasn't wearing the proper clothes for a wedding. "Friend, he asked, how is it that you are here without wedding clothes?" And the man had no reply. Then the king said to his aides, "Bind him hand and foot and throw him out into the outer darkness, where there is weeping and gnashing of teeth."
>
> - Matthew 22:11-13 (NLT)

I don't yet know the full meaning of this parable but I do understand enough to know it would be very wise to let Jesus counsel us concerning what clothes to put off and what clothes to put on. Can you say Amen?

Let me talk about Naked. That got your attention back didn't it? In **Genesis 2:25** *"the man and his wife were both naked and were not embarrassed or ashamed in each other's presence."* No sense of shame because nothing was wrong, yet.

"At that moment, their eyes were opened, and they suddenly felt shame at their nakedness. So they strung "fig leaves" together to cover themselves."

- Genesis 3:7 (NLT)

That moment was the moment man first sinned and wrongness replaced rightness in mankind. All of us were born subject to that moment ever since and we've also added to our shame by creating a few "moments" of our own, haven't we? Is that what people mean when they say, *"we all have our moments"*? Notice how quickly we try to cover up and hide our wrongness? We didn't go straight to God; we went straight to the fig leaves. That was man's first religion. First church of the fig leaves. Let's enjoy some fig leaf fellowship! We'll pretend nothing is wrong but if we hear God coming, we'll all hide.

"Adam said, I heard the sound of You [walking] in the garden, and I was afraid because I was naked; and I hid myself."

- Genesis 3:10

Rather than surrender ourselves to the mercy of God and trust Him, we proudly attempt to solve our own shame problem by covering the shame of our nakedness before God with a disguise, just like Adam's proverbial fig leaf covering. Since you asked, I'll tell you some common examples of our fig leaf coverings are religion, perfectionism, temper tantrums, verbal, emotional or physical violence, blaming others, hating self, withdrawal into hiding, self righteousness, hypocritical play acting, extreme jealousy, controlling, domineering attitudes and there are many more but I think you get the picture.

All these things are smoke screens to hide, to cover the shame we so desperately don't want revealed. But in our vanity we never stop to realize that God sees all our nakedness and He still loves us anyway. He loves us so much that even though we were too ashamed to ask, here's our merciful God just eleven verses later covering man.

Genesis 3:21 says "the Lord God made
long coats of skins and clothed them."

He is so good to us.

"Neither is there any creature that is not manifest in his sight: but all things are naked and opened unto the eyes of him with whom we have to do."

- Hebrews 4:13 (KJV)

Shame produces a constant underlying sense of wrongness which provokes and pushes us to strive after self-righteousness to cover the shame of our nakedness.

"For they being ignorant of God's righteousness, and going about to establish their own righteousness, have not submitted themselves unto the righteousness of God."

- Romans 10:3 (KJV)

The un-renewed mind of fallen man only sees the flesh; it is barely aware of even the existence of the spirit, so when the spirit gets regenerated at the new birth our soul still sees wrongness. That's why we feel naked and become ashamed. Then we get so busy trying to make ourselves appear right that we don't see how to simply cry out to Him and trust him to make us not ashamed.

"They cried to You and were delivered; they trusted in, leaned on, and confidently relied on You, and were not ashamed or confounded or disappointed."

- Psalm 22:5

If we only knew it He already took care of cleansing us from our sin and He already got rid of our guilt, and He already provided us with some beautiful new white clothes in Christ.

"He is the sole expression of the glory of God [the Light-being, the out-raying or radiance of the divine], and He is the perfect imprint and very image of [God's] nature, upholding and maintaining and guiding and propelling the universe by His mighty word of power. When He had, by offering Himself, accomplished our cleansing of sins and riddance of guilt, He sat down at the right hand of the divine Majesty on high."

- Hebrews 1:3

The work is finished. He said so on the cross. Now He is sitting down waiting for us catch on, waiting for us to get it, waiting for us to wake up to the awesome reality of what He's already done for us. If there is anything man should be ashamed of it is this; we are sleep walking right through the revealing of the most amazing gift ever given to mankind. Our first thought every day should be In the pigsty of my wrongness, You gave me the gift of the perfect rightness of Your only Son. Now that is amazing grace! But we say, *"Oh, I don't deserve that."* Of course you don't! That's what makes it all the more amazing! Wake up! Accept the gift O proud man!

"Awake to righteousness, and sin not; for some have not the knowledge of God: I speak this to your shame."

- 1 Corinthians 15:34 (KJV)

We're ashamed of the wrong things. If you insist on being ashamed, then be ashamed of being too proud to accept the price-less gift of rightness in Christ Jesus. Forgive me for repeating myself but I'm going to say that one again. If you insist on being ashamed, then be ashamed of being too proud to accept the priceless gift of rightness in Christ Jesus.

The Bible teaches in **Jeremiah 20:18** that *"man's days can be consumed by shame"*? What a waste it is for a man to allow his days to be consumed by an unnecessary sense of wrongness after God has already given him the amazing gift of rightness.

> Therefore, [there is] now no condemnation (no adjudging guilty of wrong) for those who are in Christ Jesus, who live [and] walk not after the dictates of the flesh, but after the dictates of the Spirit.
>
> - Romans 8:1

I made a statement earlier that; *"if you walk in the flesh, all you see is wrongness, in yourself, and in others. If you walk in the Spirit, you see rightness."* This is where you might ask, how do I know when I'm walking after the flesh or after the spirit? That one's easy. If you feel condemned or guilty or wrong or ashamed and you see no way out, you're in the flesh. However if you feel justified or innocent or righteous or confident every time you turn to the Lord, then you're in the Spirit because **2 Corinthians 3:16-18** says;

> "whenever a person turns [in repentance] to the Lord, the veil is stripped off and taken away. Now the Lord is the Spirit, and where the Spirit of the Lord is, there is liberty (emancipation from bondage, freedom). And all of us, as with unveiled face, [because we] continued to behold [in the Word of God] as in a mirror the glory of the Lord, are constantly being transfigured into His very

own image in ever increasing splendor and from one degree of glory to another; [for this comes] from the Lord [Who is] the Spirit."

And again it is written in **Psalm 34:22**;

"The Lord redeems the lives of His servants, and none of those who take refuge and trust in Him shall be condemned or held guilty."

Our life is in Him or else we remain, abide in death and not in life. You are in Him by hearing, and then doing whatever He says. He says to acknowledge our wrongness, not hide it and to confess our sin, not try to cover it up.

"I acknowledged my sin to You, and my iniquity I did not hide. I said, I will confess my transgressions to the Lord [continually unfolding the past till all is told]—"then" You [instantly] forgave me the guilt and iniquity of my sin. Selah [pause, and calmly think on that]!"

- Psalm 32:5

"If we confess our sins, he is faithful and just to forgive us our sins, and to cleanse us from all unrighteousness."

- 1st John 1:9 (KJV)

What if we refuse to confess? Scary!

"Confess your faults one to another, and pray one for another, that ye may be healed. The effectual fervent prayer of a righteous man availeth much."

- James 5:16 (KJV)

So who is the righteous man? Glad you asked! He is the man who just confessed sin and got cleansed of all unrighteousness so all that's left in him is the rightness of Christ.

> "Then said I, Woe is me! For I am undone and ruined, because I am a man of unclean lips, and I dwell in the midst of a people of unclean lips; for my eyes have seen the King, the Lord of hosts! Then flew one of the seraphim [heavenly beings] to me, having a live coal in his hand which he had taken with tongs from off the altar; And with it he touched my mouth and said, Behold, this has touched your lips; your iniquity and guilt are taken away, and your sin is completely atoned for and forgiven. Also I heard the voice of the Lord, saying, Whom shall I send? And who will go for Us? Then said I, Here am I; send me."
>
> - Isaiah 6:5-7

Did you catch that transformation church? In verse 5 he is ruined because he sees how clean God is, and by comparison, how dirty he is. But God sends Holy Spirit refining fire to him the moment he confesses his uncleanness and by verse 8 he has transformed from *"woe is me"* to *"Here am I, send me!"* Go and do likewise church. Stop hiding and confess. It will turn out much better than you could ever imagine.

2nd Corinthians 4:2 says men hide through shame and it goes on to reveal the way out of the hiding habit is to state the truth openly, clearly and candidly. After hearing all this if you still feel a need to hide then at least trust God to hide you in Christ rather than trust you to hide in yourself. The safest place in all creation is the secret place of the Most High spoken of in **Psalm 91** and you get there by trust in Christ. The way "out" of shame is to be "in" Christ.

"For [as far as this world is concerned] you have died, and your [new, real] life is hidden with Christ in God."

- Colossians 3:3

You begin to be hidden in Christ by surrendering all your own self protection methods, like hiding and blaming, and simply trusting that He will do a better job of protecting and clothing you than you could ever hope to. You need to be covered with the humility of Christ, rather than the pride of man. You've been so busy covering yourself that God can't cover you.

1st Peter 5:5 says to "clothe yourselves with humility as the garb of a servant, so that its covering cannot possibly be stripped from you, with freedom from pride and arrogance toward one another. For God sets Himself against the proud but gives grace to the humble."

We need to embrace humility but many of us trust in pride by either taking too much responsibility on our self or placing all the blame on others and accept no responsibility on our self. Some people fluctuate back and forth between the two extremes not realizing that both extremes are false. The common denominator here is a focus on self which always ensures we will get it wrong because we see everything as it relates to the "false god" of me, myself and I. We can only see accurately when we look at a situation from the viewpoint of Christ. This life is simply not about us. It's all about Him and the sooner we learn that, the easier everything becomes.

God and the devil have one thing in common in that they both want to kill us. The word of God says repeatedly we need to let the old man be crucified with Christ. We must decrease so He can increase. That's the only way the new creation can come forth. Shame is a false image to hide behind. Mike Bickle says *"a negotiating spirit of legalism grows out of shame."*

We argue with God and His representatives and attempt to negotiate a degree of acceptable self-righteousness because of all our many mighty wonderful works under the "law of perfect performance" but in clinging to a righteousness of our own, we completely miss the grace of God and are therefore doomed to be ultimately rejected.

> "Not everyone who says to Me, Lord, Lord, will enter the kingdom of heaven, but he who does the will of My Father Who is in heaven. 22 Many will say to Me on that day, Lord, Lord, have we not prophesied in Your name and driven out demons in Your name and done many mighty works in Your name? 23 And then I will say to them openly (publicly), I never knew you; depart from Me, you who act wickedly [disregarding My commands]."

> - Matthew 7:21-23

Oh please church! Let's humble ourselves and
do what we're told. Father really does know best.

Let me share a wonderful testimony that clearly illustrates much of what I've been saying here. The testimony of Judy in her own words.

> "Recently I was led to confess a sin before my brethren but had been reluctant to disclose it because I was afraid of the way they might view me after I did so. However, since my fear of the Lord is increasing and my fear of man decreasing, I found the strength to do what I thought I could never do and confessed it anyway. At first I was relieved to get it out in the open and it felt good to be obedient to God. The response from my brethren was not at all what I feared it would be, but instead they immediately loved and encouraged me.

However, what happened after that was a slow and steady decline into what I call a pit of shame. Thoughts started coming to me, that after their initial acceptance of me following my confession, everyone would have time to think about it, and would now start wondering what else I was hiding and wondering whether I was trustworthy. There was a crack in the mask that I had hid behind all my life and now they could see behind the mask. I had learned how to live fairly normal in my shameful wrongness by building up a socially acceptable mask or facade, but now that they could see me behind the mask, I could not function.

The feeling of wrongness grew and I found myself beginning to criticize and fault find with my family members to compensate for the intensifying sense of wrongness. The feelings that I was a fraud, an imposter, a fake were overwhelming. I continued to feel more and more exposed, like a sudden and unexpected nakedness and over several days I had withdrawn to the point that I couldn't bear talking to anybody.

On the morning of the 6th day into this process my husband Victor, feeling a little helpless by now and knowing I have respect for the word of God, tried to use scripture to get me to snap out of it. Although normally this would work, this time it just felt like he was beating me with scripture. Then the next morning, feeling helpless and rejected, Victor just withdrew from me completely, which made me feel abandoned in the pit.

Feeling desperate to be in harmony with my husband the way we usually are, I said to him "sometimes we can use scripture to help people get out of their situation and sometimes we just need to walk away for awhile, but there are also times when we must lay down our comfort and go in to where they are to bring them out." He asked "what can I do for you"? I said "I don't know, just don't leave me in this place alone"?

Victor then said "whatever it takes, for as long as it takes, I'll do it." In the love that I felt at that moment when Victor laid down his life for me, I heard God say to me in the most loving way "I know who you are." "Nevertheless, I don't condemn you, I accept you anyway." I was immediately flooded with a sense of love and acceptance and felt some relief for the first time that week. I recalled the following two scriptures:

"When Jesus had lifted up himself, and saw none but the woman, he said unto her, Woman, where are your accusers? Has no man condemned thee? She said, No man, Lord. And Jesus said unto her, Neither do I condemn thee: go, and sin no more."

- John 8:10-11

Where are your accusers? Ask the same question of yourself. For many of us our chief accuser is our self, with "help" from those of our own household. Forgive yourself, and them, because they don't know what they're doing any more than you do.

"And, behold, a woman in the city, which was a sinner, when she knew that Jesus sat at meat in the Pharisee's house, brought an alabaster box of ointment, And stood at his feet behind him weeping, and began to wash his feet with tears, and did wipe them with the hairs of her head, and kissed his feet, and anointed them with the ointment. Now when the Pharisee which had bidden him saw it, he spoke within himself, saying, This man, if he were a prophet, would have known who and what manner of woman this is that touches him: for she is a sinner. And Jesus answering said unto him, Simon, I have somewhat to say unto thee. And he saith, Master, say on. There was a certain creditor which had two debtors: the one owed five hundred pence, and the other fifty. And when they had nothing to pay, he frankly forgave them both. Tell me therefore, which of them will love him most? Simon answered and said, I suppose that he, to whom he forgave most. And he said unto him, Thou hast rightly judged. And he turned to the woman, and said unto Simon, See thou this woman? I entered into thine house, thou gavest me no water for my feet: but she hath washed my feet with tears, and wiped them with the hairs of her head. Thou gavest me no kiss: but this woman since the time I came in hath not ceased to kiss my feet. My head with oil thou didst not anoint: but this woman hath anointed my feet with ointment. Wherefore I say unto thee, Her sins, which are many, are forgiven; for she loved much: but to whom little is forgiven, the same loveth little. And he said unto her, Thy sins are forgiven. And they that sat at meat with him began to say within themselves, Who is this that forgiveth sins also? And he said to the woman, Thy faith hath saved thee; go in peace."

- Luke 7:37-50

Testimony of Judy concluded:

Later on the evening of the 7th day, when the house was quiet, God spoke to me "there is no one good but God, no not one." The understanding was that we have all sinned, we are all born "bad" because of this sin nature, the only time we are "good" is when God, who alone is good, does good through us. Because the entrance of God's truth brings light into the darkness of our understanding, I began to realize for the first time in my life that I am not a mistake, there is nothing wrong with me when I make a mistake or say something wrong, I have nothing to be ashamed of, I'm ok, I'm free! Thank you Jesus!

Psalm 53:1 says "there are none who do good."

Romans 3:9-12 says "that all men, both Jews and Greeks (Gentiles), are under sin [held down by and subject to its power and control]. As it is written, None is righteous, just and truthful and upright and conscientious, no, not one. No one understands [no one intelligently discerns or comprehends]; no one seeks out God. All have turned aside; together they have gone wrong and have become unprofitable and worthless; no one does right, not even one!"

Psalm 14:1-3 says "there is none that does good or right, They are all gone aside, they have all together become filthy; there is none that does good or right, no, not one."

In **Matthew 19:17** Jesus said unto him, "Why callest thou me good? there is none good but one, that is, God" again in Mark 10:18 "Jesus said unto him, Why callest thou me good? there is none good but one, that is, God."

We all have the spiritual birth defect of sin. Yet again in **Luke 18:19** Jesus said *"Why do you call Me good? No one is good—except God only."* Humans think, and our religions imply, that if we can just do "good," we are a good person and if we do "bad" we are a bad person. But since all good and perfect gifts come from the Lord, as **James 1:16** says, then when we do good it's from Jesus, and when we do bad it's from Adam, it's the evil sin nature that has been ever present with us since Eden.

"For I know that nothing good dwells within me, that is, in my flesh. I can will what is right, but I cannot perform it. [I have the intention and urge to do what is right, but no power to carry it out.] For I fail to practice the good deeds I desire to do, but the evil deeds that I do not desire to do are what I am [ever] doing. Now if I do what I do not desire to do, it is no longer I doing it it is not myself that acts], but the sin [principle] which dwells within me [fixed and operating in my soul]. So I find it to be a law (rule of action of my being) that when I want to do what is right and good, evil is ever present with me and I am subject to its insistent demands."

- Romans 7:18-21

We must learn to separate what we do, from who we are. We are a new creation being shaped and formed into the image of Christ, and at the same time the old sin man is being crucified one battle at a time. It is an ongoing war within us between good and evil. It is nothing to be ashamed of when we lose one of the battles. We are all going through it but only One Man ever performed perfectly and He died for you, so just accept that. Simply accept the reality that you are not God, you're not perfect and in fact, you're not even good. Just accept that. Quit trying to make yourselves something that you're just not.

Scripture asks in **Jeremiah 13:23** "Can the Ethiopian change his skin or the leopard his spots? Then also can you do good who are accustomed and taught [even trained] to do evil?"

Jesus himself said in **Luke 11:13** that we are evil but God loves us and he doesn't leave us in our shame, guilt and sinful wrongness. He loves us so much that He sent His perfect Son to take our shameful life upon Himself at the cross and then God gave Jesus' glorious life to shameful man at the resurrection. However, we cannot live the glorious righteous life of being Christ-like new creations while we're simultaneously trying to cling to our old, unregenerate shameful sinful life. Would you bring a rotten old stinking corpse to your wedding? Of course not! Then let's quit trying to bring the old unregenerate man that we used to be, dead in his trespass and sins to Jesus's wedding.

God says in **Hosea 4:6** His people are destroyed for lack of knowledge and that is still true today. We say that we are in Christ but we don't live like we are in Christ. The Holy Spirit once told me that if Christians would simply believe and live just one verse it would completely and totally and radically transform them into Christ likeness practically overnight. Put your ears on and snap to full attention and I'll tell you that one verse. Bring your faith right up to the front of your thinking. Are you ready? Here is the verse.

"Therefore, if anyone is in Christ, he is a new creation. The old has passed away; behold, the new has come."

- 2 Corinthians 5:17 (ESV)

If we really believed that old things are passed away and that all things are new then our lives would transform miraculously into the image and likeness of Christ. The problem is we still think that we are, who we were. We still think that we are, what we do. And we cling desperately, like our life depends on it, to our old nature and our old way of thinking and behaving and speaking but unless we are willing to lose that life, we are never able to put on the life of the new creation. We talk about the new birth and the new creation all the time, we just don't live it because the idolatrous false god of Me, Myself and I is too busy wallowing in the past and worrying and doubting about the future.

The Bible teaches us to forget yesterday and quit worrying about tomorrow. Today, while it is still called today, renew your mind to the truth of God's Word. **Romans 12:2** says if you renew your mind, it will transform your life. The old man that you were, deserved to die on the cross, which he did, in Christ, 2000 years ago. Will you just let him go? Clinging to who you "were," is killing who you "are."

Jesus said in **Matthew 16:25** "whoever is bent on saving his [temporal] life [his comfort and security here] shall lose it [eternal life]; and whoever loses his life [his comfort and security here] for My sake shall find it [life everlasting]."

Give up the false comfort of your old mind rut. We're clinging to the wrong rope church. Believe your heart, not your head. Walk by faith, not by sight as **2nd Corinthians 5:7** advises. You should read **2nd Corinthians 5:14-21** and weep out loud for joy. God has made me Christ's ambassador and He is making His appeal as it were through me.

As a personal representative of Christ I beg you for His sake to lay hold of the divine favor [now offered you] and be reconciled to God by the renewal of your mind so you can prove, by the way you live your life, what is the good and perfect and acceptable will of God, right here, right now, on the earth, in this life, demonstrating the new creation to everyone you meet and thereby reflecting the hopefulness of God's glory into the faces of all the shame slaves you meet. Having been set free, you can now be used by God to set others free by telling them and demonstrating to them that this life is not the life. This temporal life on earth is the embryonic stage where our choices are used by our Creator to shape and form us for our real, eternal life which can actually start here, if we let it.

In **Deuteronomy 30:19** God calls heaven and earth to witness that He has set before us life and death, the blessings and the curses; then He gives us a big hint, *"choose life"* that we and our descendants may live and may love the Lord our God, obey His voice, and cling to Him. For He is our life and the length of our days. Amazing! God is both pro life and pro choice. He advises us to choose life and He sends His Son to die, that we might have the choice to live, eternally. What an awesome God we serve!

Christ took all our shame, guilt and condemnation upon Himself at the cross, and it killed Him. But God raised Him from the dead to walk in newness of life with no more shame, no more guilt and no more condemnation because the penalty for those things is death and He already paid the full price so all shame is gone and He is a new creation. If you can grasp that our shame was put on Him at the cross then by the same principle you should be able to grasp that His glory was put on you at the resurrection. If He can receive your wrongness and it killed Him then you should be able to grasp that we received His rightness, and it made us alive, in the new creation!

Oh please church! Do you see that? It is the essence of Christianity but many Christians don't know it or they wouldn't think like they think, they wouldn't live like they live. They see it for a brief moment and open their hearts to receive His Seed but then the growth is choked and stifled because it's so hard for them to get the reality of the new creation out from their spirit and into their soul. Their mind is very slow to renew and therefore the transformation is stunted.

The carnal mind is enmity against God and can never learn these things on it's own but, God has established an order and it is this: your mind will submit to, and can be renewed by your reborn spirit. However, this is exactly the process that shame hinders and complicates. This is an excellent reason to reject the grave clothes of shame because they dwell in the dividing line between soul and spirit, spoken of in **Hebrews 4:12**, and create a block, a disconnect, so the truth, the reality, of the new birth that your brand new spirit knows very well, can't easily, or can't at all, get through to your soul, thereby effectively hindering and even stopping the transformation from who you were, to who you are.

This is a hopeless and impossible dilemma with man yet Jesus said in **Mark 10:27** *"with God, all things are possible"* but again, God has an order. First you plant seed, then you eat of the harvest. The spiritual law here is called sowing and reaping.

Let me explain how it applies to this situation. Blame produces shame and shame produces more blame and this cycle just keeps spinning out of control. It's like deliberately spreading weed seeds in your garden and then wondering why you have so little good fruit and so many thorns and thistles. Shame and blame feed each other while starving out righteousness and justification.

Do you want to be justified? Then justify the person next to you and just watch God's law of sowing and reaping cause you to be justified. Do you want to be condemned? Simply blame the person next to you and watch God's law of sowing and reaping cause you to be guilty and ashamed. It's amazingly simple. You plant it. You harvest it. You dish it out. You will eat it up. What goes around comes around. You need only look back over your life to see this process is exactly what's been going on all of your life.

If you want to harvest a different crop you have to plant a different seed. Your words are the seeds of your future. What you plant today, you eat tomorrow. You blame them today, you'll be guilty tomorrow. It doesn't take a rocket scientist to figure out how to change this cycle. Even the littlest disciple of the Lord Jesus Christ can begin to change it in a moment of time. Begin immediately to justify the person next to you and look for ways to make them right and watch how fast God justifies you and makes you righteous. Not only in His sight, but even in yours! Go ahead and try it. You have nothing to lose but your old life and you weren't totally thrilled with that life anyway.

"Let no corrupting talk (seed) come out of your mouths, but only such as is good for building up, as fits the occasion, that it may give grace to those who hear."

- Ephesians 4:29 (ESV)

"Understand [this], my beloved brethren. Let every man be quick to hear (seed selection time) [a ready listener], slow to speak (think before you plant), slow to take offense and to get angry."

- James 1:19

In **Matthew 7:1** Jesus says if you don't judge and criticize and condemn others, you won't be judged and criticized and condemned yourself. In other words, you give grace and mercy to them, so you get grace and mercy. If you refuse to release them, you're toast. **Matthew 7:2** says exactly the way you dish it out to others, that's exactly the way it will be fed to you. How can anyone ever say God is unfair? He is giving us just what we're asking for?

There is another aspect of this transference of rightness and wrongness that we need to realize. Just as we see that Christ took our wrongness on Himself and gave us His rightness, so also should we, as His body, His ambassadors, be willing to suffer others putting their wrongness on us. However be sure to do this from the position that the wrongness is just passing through you to Christ, you were never expected to hold that wrongness. This is the law of Christ, submit to it, don't fight back, don't even defend yourself. Jesus is your Defender. If they dump their wrongness on you and demand that you carry it for a mile, do it. And do it with a good attitude, as though you were doing it for Christ, because you are! Carry their burden for a mile, carry it for two miles, but don't carry it forever and do cast the care of it up to Jesus at the first opportunity. Resist the temptation to appoint yourself to be "God's little martyr."

> "Bear (endure, carry) one another's burdens and troublesome moral faults, and in this way fulfill and observe perfectly the law of Christ (the Messiah) and complete what is lacking [in your obedience to it]. For if any person thinks himself to be somebody [too important to condescend to shoulder another's load] when he is nobody [of superiority except in his own estimation, (aka pride)], he deceives and deludes and cheats himself."

> - Galatians 6:2-3

So you see that putting blame on others is the exact opposite of the law of Christ because as you just heard in **Galatians 6:2-3**, our job is to take it from them. It's a little mini version of what Christ did for us on the cross.

Let me talk about the link between shame and the idolatry of self, better known as PRIDE. *"I will exalt myself"* is the motto of pride but it disguises itself in subtle and clever ways. We think of pride saying *"I'm really hot stuff,"* which it does, but pride also says *"I'm a total low life loser"* also known as the wrongness mask of "worm theology" that I mentioned in the start of this message. Both extremes are equally wrong and they are both pride because they both deny and defy the truth of God's word which says in **1st Corinthians 15:10** *"I am what I am by the grace of God."*

Humility says *"I am whatever God says I am."* Some of us say that "I'm good" to cover up how bad I really feel about myself and inversely some of us say "I'm really bad" to cover up that God has totally cleansed me of bad and He has made me good but *I* can't accept that either because *I* have whatever *I* think promoted way over anyone else's opinion, including God's opinion.

In **Job 40:8** God asks a question of Job, "Will you also annul (set aside and render void) My judgment? Will you condemn Me [your God], that you may [appear] righteous and justified?"

Jesus said when you do it to them, you do it to Me. See how shame gets its power from pride because shame and pride both agree together to defy and to doubt God's Word. God has given us a spectacular and miraculous new birth and new identity in Christ, but many people cannot believe who they are in Christ. They cannot embrace their new identity because of their unbelief which is rooted in shame and shame has its root in pride. The unbelief is fed and sustained by a root of shame.

If a man will humble himself to the truth of God's word, that will uproot the shame lie, and now he is free to believe who he is in Christ. God says you're justified, shame says you're condemned. God says He made you right by the blood of Christ but shame says you're still wrong. God says you're free because Jesus paid your sin ransom but shame says you're still the slave of sin. Pride and shame constantly attempt to exalt themselves to the position of God and even higher if they're allowed to. They have no chance of success before God but if *you* allow them to, they will exalt their words over God's words in your life, in your understanding, which you shouldn't be leaning to anyway. Adam and Eve knew that God said *"you eat it and you will die."* The devil said you won't die.

In their pride they believe the lie more than the truth and they ended up naked, ashamed and dead. It didn't have to be that way. They only needed to humble themselves to the truth of God's Word.

That's all you and I need to do. Humility says I am what God says I am. God said it and that settles it. With that in mind, let me close this message by reading to you from God's Word what He says about your shame guilt and condemnation. Open your ears.

Ephesians 5:26 speaks of being "washed with the water of the Word" and Jesus said in **John 15:3** "You are clean through the word which I have spoken unto you."

I'm going to speak several *"no shame allowed"* verses in your hearing right now and I ask that you purpose, allow and expect these verses to flow over and clean you right now. Let him who has ears, hear what the Spirit saith to the churches.

"he who believes in Jesus [who adheres to, TRUSTS in, and relies on Him] shall never be disappointed or put to shame."

- 1 Peter 2:6

"you were washed clean (purified by a complete atonement for sin and made free from the guilt of sin), and you were consecrated (set apart, hallowed), and you were justified [pronounced righteous, by TRUSTING] in the name of the Lord Jesus Christ and in the [Holy] Spirit of our God."

- 1 Corinthians 6:11

"let none who trust and wait hopefully and look for You be put to shame or be disappointed"

- Psalm 25:3

"he who believes in Him [who adheres to, TRUSTS in, and relies on Him] shall not be put to shame nor be disappointed in his expectations."

- Romans 9:33

Praise God! You ought to be feeling pretty clean by now. Please notice that all of these verses require us to trust our God. We will not be put to shame because we trust in Jesus with childlike faith. If you haven't heard the recorded message on TRUST yet, you should. I'm going to stop at this point and leave you washed by the living water of the word of Almighty God. Shame is a severe bondage in the church today so there will be a part two of this message very soon.

Heavenly Father, I pray that You will seal these words in your servants and cause all those who received these words to "come forth" and have their grave clothes removed that they may serve You in white clothes and that they may walk upright before You in newness of life, free of shame, guilt and condemnation, for I ask it in Jesus Name. Amen!

<u>Notes</u>

**Scan this QR code to
listen to part two.
Or visit *thevoiceoftruth.net***

Part Two

Behold, the new has come...

"So if the Son sets you free, you will be free indeed."

- John 8:36 (ESV)

In part one, I used the metaphor of Lazarus coming out of his burial cave, but even though he was free of death, he was still unable to live life abundantly because he was bound head to foot with grave clothes. Jesus commanded in **John 11:44** *"remove the grave clothes and let him go."*

Several years ago as I was ministering to a man, I saw a vision of this man completely bound, like a mummy, but there was a small opening where the grave wrappings didn't quite cover his right eye fully, and through that small opening the man's spirit viewed all his experiences, and through that same small opening I was enabled in this vision to see inside the mummy where a small boy, perhaps 5 or 6 years old, was repeatedly jumping up from within the hollow shell of the mummy to catch glimpses through the eye opening. The little boy was trying to see the reality going on outside all around the mummy.

That mummy was the older person that nearly everyone in this man's entire life had interacted with. But here is the shocking part of the vision. The small boy leaping to see out through the opening of the man's right eye, that small boy was the real person! The mummy of the outer man was a carefully arranged facade, an outer shell that the man had developed over a lifetime to protect and hide the vulnerable little boy, his true identity.

I understood that the outer shell that everyone interacted with was the man's soul, especially his intellect, his mind. And I realized the small hidden boy was the man's heart and at that moment

I understood why it was so rare that anyone got to interact with, or touch his heart, his spirit, because it was so elaborately bound up and hidden. It required repeated and extraordinary effort for the hidden boy of the heart to leap up to the uncovered eye which was like a very high small window to the spirit.

On the rare occasions where others were privileged to interact with the heart of the man, it was totally thrilling and created great hope for a growing heart to heart communion in the next meeting. Sadly, the next time we met, it was as though the last heart to heart communication had never happened. So the oneness of heart to heart communion could not grow. It just seemed to start and then disappear by the next meeting.

Now I have come to understand that the extraordinary effort that it took for the little boy to get up to the small opening in the grave clothes was totally exhausting and the boy would simply curl up in a ball and sleep like a prisoner, totally drained of strength by his extreme efforts to escape or at least see out of his dungeon. Often the boy never showed up a single time at most interactions so our conversation could only be about religion, politics, weather or some subject matter the intellect of the mummy could converse on. There was no heart to heart possible because the hidden boy of the heart was nowhere to be found. Over time he would just surrender his hope to the loneliness that only a heart can feel, and just go numb, like he didn't exist.

Some of you listening to these words right now understand exactly what I am saying. And you see a light shining into the high window. That Light is Jesus and He will not only rekindle your faint hope but He will flood the mummy with light inside by calling you forth out of your dark cave of hopelessness with His voice. Even more, His words entering into your heart right now will make His Light so bright that it will melt away the grave clothes of your shame as you come out. You are the reason God had us make this message. He did it for you! These words are His words and the entrance of His word gives Light. You don't even have to wait another moment to start coming free. Just open your mouth right now by crying out *"here I am Jesus!" "I want to come out!" "I want to be free!" "I want to be one with You right now!"*

Romans 10:13 says, *"For whosoever shall call upon the name of the Lord shall be saved."* Release your faith by calling out His name right now. Start walking by faith, right out of the darkness and don't believe a single doubting thought. Tell the lies to *"get out in Jesus Name"* and if the lie doesn't seem to leave, then call out loud to Jesus right now and say *"Jesus, this stinking lie thinks it can stay after I ordered it to go in Your name!" "Will You take care of it for me Lord?"*

I tell you the truth, the instant Jesus so much as looks at it, that lie doesn't have as good a chance as the proverbial snowball in hell. Now don't stop coming out and don't bother looking back in doubt. You continue coming out by continuing to follow the instructions contained in Truth.

> So Jesus said to those Jews who had believed in Him, If you abide in My word [hold fast to My teachings and live in accordance with them], you are truly My disciples. And you will know the Truth, and the Truth will set you free.
>
> - John 8:31-32

Some people really want it spelled out for them so I'll lay it out in progressive steps for you as He did for me. And I'll explain each step as we go...

STEP ONE

Strip off the old man and *then* put on Christ.

Don't try to cover grave clothes with white robes. Don't try to cover shame with Christ. Renew your mind. Don't just attempt to mask your old way of thinking with a churchy veneer. Don't try to put your new white robes on over the nasty old grave clothes. It stinketh. Change the way you see yourself. Humble your opinion of you and submit your identity to Gods opinion of you. Satan invented identity theft and you may be a victim. The only way you will ever find out who and what you really are, is to ask God. God is always right and all other opinions that differ from God, are simply wrong. Humility lets God be true and every other opinion is a liar, as **Romans 3:4** says.

When you have a wrongness mentality instead of a rightness mentality, you start each day scanning your thoughts, looking for the last place you were wrong and you go back there in your perception of yourself because that is the last place you were in a familiar, and over time, a comfortable place. Humans find a comfort in their familiar ruts and even in their familiar pits. After being set free the Israelites wanted to go back to Egypt even though they were miserable slaves there. That's where their inner beliefs were lined up with their outer evidence. People subject to shame actually look for ways to get themselves into difficulty so they can rationalize the slide back down into their familiar rut. This demonic process completely eliminates God from your equation and effectively seals you in familiar shame, wrapped up, once again, in wrongness.

God says your only evidence should be God's word, but a person can't receive truth when they've fallen into an episode of shame. To you it's as though you have been caught nearly naked and someone is trying to talk you out of your last fig leaf. You may resist furiously to avoid being found completely naked and having your wrongness fully exposed. If you are ministering to a person who has fallen into a shame pit, don't beat them with scripture and don't desert them. This is a time for love which never fails. Love is first of all patient and **Proverbs 10:12** says love covers sin and wrongness.

Just be lovingly patient and wait for them to feel their nakedness covered by His love, flowing through you. Then they will have ears to hear truth, and now you can help them get out, and stay out of the shame pit. If you now realize that you are a prisoner of shame please know that shame can't recognize shame, because it's all darkness, and darkness can't see darkness. People who are still prisoners themselves, can only commiserate with you. If they knew the way out, they would be free themselves, wouldn't they? Seek out people who walk in the Light, because they can reflect Light into the darkness of your shame. People who are free, can free you.

STEP TWO

Understand how you got this way so that after you get free, you don't ignorantly wander right back into the same bondage.

We can have shame because it was passed down from our parents, dating all the way back to the original shame in Eden. We can also have shame because of events in our life. We can have shame because of lies we have believed as true. Classic examples of this would be the child who believes their parents' divorce is somehow the child's fault. Or the child who is molested by a trusted adult and the child somehow thinks it was all their fault or the rape victim that thinks they are to blame or the beat up wife or child that believes *"I must have provoked the violence"* and on and on. Many shame victims fall into this group and they need to hunt down the source event, identify the lie, and kill it with the sword of the spirit. Cut off its ugly head and carry it around all day like David did Goliath.

Another way shame comes into your life is through the people you spend time with. Husband wife, brother, sister, friend; Jesus said in **Matthew 10:36** your enemies would be those of your own household. The people are not the source of the hostility towards us but they do unknowingly allow their mouths to be used as the enemy's bow to shoot the devils fiery arrows at us from close range. We must learn to use the full armor of God from Ephesians six and especially the shield of faith.

Listen to **Ephesians 6:16** (NET) "taking up the shield of faith with which you can extinguish all the flaming arrows of the evil one."

The Holy Spirit may lead you at times to minimize and even abstain from communication with some people until they change, or you grow strong enough to bear it, or both, because God designed man to reflect what he faces, what he sets his focus on.

"As in water, face answers to and
reflects face, so the heart of man to man."

- Proverbs 27:19

What's in your heart, shows in your life, and it reflects onto others. What's in their heart shows in their life and it reflects onto you. For example, a child looking into the eyes of their shamed parent will see the wrongness of shame looking back, reflected back, onto them self and will think the wrongness is them! Children are very discerning and will sense the shame and take the blame onto themselves. Thus shame has just been passed to the next generation. The bad news is, shame reflects shame so two shame victims will intensify each other's shame.

The good news is, a person full of God's glory can reflect the light of that glory into the darkness of your shame and you can then see the way out, the way of escape. Spend time around such people.

Listen when they speak. Do what they tell you and in due season God's glory will shine into every little corner of your darkness and then you too will become a person full of God's glory. Now there is an inheritance we want to leave for our children, so determine that shame ends right here, right now! A final note on this reflecting concept; the greater will have more influence on the lesser. In other words if you're wimpy about your faith and they are strong about their unbelief, you better leave.

While much of your shame was developed in your lifetime and inherited through your parents, please don't lose sight of what the scriptures reveal about the origin of shame. Adam and Eve were the only shame free humans on earth and they did something *wrong,* which led to *shame* which led to *hiding* which led to *blaming* and every human since then, except One, was conceived in shame and sin. Read this part carefully. Everything that came into mankind through Adam at the fall, was taken out of man at the cross. All the things Adam allowed *into* us at the fall, Jesus carried *away from* us on His cross. So why do we still feel naked and ashamed? Because lies and lack of knowledge are used by satan to steal, kill and destroy our inheritance in Christ.

Recognize and reject the lies. When I say lies, I'm not talking about the validity of the "facts" of your life. Lies are everything that is not the Truth of God's word. Live the Truth. Put on Christ. First we inherited wrongness grave clothes from Adam then we inherited rightness God clothes from Jesus. God gave us robes of righteousness; don't allow yourself to be defrauded out of the gift. God says you are not who you were and you are not what you were. You are not naked and ashamed anymore so you don't need to hide. Adam sinned in the garden and when he saw his nakedness (by nakedness, I mean his wrongness was exposed) he was ashamed and his response was to try and hide it and blame Eve; one hand on the fig leaf and the other hand pointing at his wife.

Shame brings blame and hiding. Shame leads to fear of being exposed and found out. This fear, like all fears, creates bondage. You become imprisoned by fear. The Lord told my wife that *"Shame is the accusation that puts us in prison, and our fear over having our wrongness exposed (naked) is the power that **keeps** us in prison."*

Over our lifetime we develop more and more elaborate and complex methods to hide and disguise our shame and all this to cover up something that probably wasn't even our fault and in some cases it didn't even happen. The original charge was not even true! We've spent a lifetime in bondage to the fear of men seeing our wrongness. Imprisoned by the fear of being caught naked we allow our lives to be controlled by shamefully hiding something that's not even real! Let me give you an example of what I'm saying.

> Early in the morning Abraham took some food and a skin of water and gave them to Hagar. He put them on her shoulders, gave her the child, and sent her away. So she went wandering aimlessly through the wilderness of Beer Sheba. When the water in the skin was gone, she shoved the child under one of the shrubs. Then she went and sat down by herself across from him at quite a distance, about a bowshot away; for she thought, "I refuse to watch the child die." So she sat across from him and wept uncontrollably.
>
> - Genesis 21:14-16 (NET)

So here's a young boy, Ishmael, rejected by Sarah because she loved her son Isaac more. Rejected by his dad Abraham because Sarah is railing on him to get rid of this kid. Rejected by his own mom Hagar because she decides he's gonna die and she can't bear to watch it. Now you tell me; does this boy Ishmael have some serious rejection issues? Every adult in his life appears to reject this boy. Big time. But it's not because of his mistakes, it's because of theirs. Is any of this his fault? No. Did he do anything wrong to deserve this rejection? No. Nevertheless, he probably grew up hostile and violent to hide and disguise the deeply ingrained sense that something must be shamefully wrong with him to be so completely rejected.

Yet none of this was even his fault. The stage was set before he was even born.

It gets worse. He unknowingly passed on this deep sense of shame to his descendants and by example taught them to hide shame behind violence and hostility to this very day. One of Ishmael's descendants is Osama Bin Laden. All the facts of this sad case point to a seemingly unsolvable problem. Certainly we humans have not been able to resolve the Arab/Israeli issue to this day; that's a historical fact. But God's truth overrules mans facts, *if we believe it.* And the truth in this case is that Almighty God had never rejected Ishmael.

In **Genesis 21:13** God told Abraham, "I will also make the son of the slave wife into a great nation, for he (Ishmael) is your descendant too."

Now read this part carefully...None of this mess had to be this way! The truth is both the sons were accepted, *if they only believed it.*

Let me read you the account of Cain and Abel in **Genesis 4:7** from the amplified Bible.

"If you do well, will you not be accepted? And if you do not do well, sin crouches at your door; its desire is for you, but you must master it."

- Genesis 4:7

Cain held resentment towards his brother Abel because, in his view, Abel was accepted and Cain viewed himself as rejected and the "facts" seemed to confirm this view but God said to Cain, *"If you do well, will you not be accepted?"* This is a very important spiritual truth. **Deuteronomy 30:19** says God set before man the choice between life and death and between good and evil (evil in scripture is defined as everything that is "not good"). The very next verse (**Gen. 4:8**) says Cain promptly went out and murdered Abel. We'd have to define this choice as "not good," aka evil.

God gave Cain a chance to give up his bitter resentment towards Abel but Cain chose to pass up his opportunity to do well and thereby be accepted. Instead Cain chose to obey sin and sin thereby mastered him. **Romans 6:16** says whoever you continue to obey, that becomes your master and **Luke 16:13** says no man can serve two masters so Cain traded masters when he obeyed sin. He resented his brother more than he loved God. He loved the feeling of hatred towards his brother more than he loved God. He loved evil more than good. He rejected doing good and thereby caused his own rejection because he changed masters; he changed gods.

Man strives to blame someone else for our wrong choices but in reality, we caused our own rejection as surely as Cain and Ishmael caused their own rejection and so began lifetimes and even generations of wrongness being hidden behind the grave clothes of shame. At any point along the way we can simply choose to believe God's truth, which is doing well in Gods sight. Then we will be accepted and there's no longer anything to hide because God has made us right in Christ. Believe it or not, that is the question.

> He who believes in Him [who clings to, trusts in, relies on Him] is not judged [he who trusts in Him never comes up for judgment; for him there is no rejection, no condemnation—he incurs no damnation]; but he who does not believe (cleave to, rely on, trust in Him) is judged already [he has already been convicted and has already received his sentence] because he has not believed in and trusted in the name of the only begotten Son of God. [He is condemned for refusing to let his trust rest in Christ's name.]

> - John 3:18

The only thing really wrong with any of us is that we don't believe God. The day we believe God, our wrongness problem is solved. Nothing was really wrong with Cain or Ishmael that the truth couldn't resolve. But they didn't seek or welcome the truth; instead they fell for the lie. If someone else appeared to be favored over them, then the whispered dark lie came subtly and said, *"There must be something wrong with you and that's why someone else appeared more accepted than you."*

They began to see everything through this wrongness filter and increasingly came to see themselves as the wrong sons and therefore rejected. Shamed by the rejection, they began a lifestyle of hiding and blaming not realizing that the darkness of shame is the perfect growing environment for evil. So hate, pride, envy, selfishness and all the fruit of the flesh can now grow in the dark hiding place created by shame. Shame is a greenhouse for evil. The way of escape is to repent of all the sin and then turn from the guilt and condemnation that allow shame to grow and get stronger. Starve it out. Don't feed the monster. Do some rejecting of your own. Truthfully and forcefully reject out loud the lie that created the shame in the first place. God has not rejected you. God loves you so much he gave Jesus for you. You are accepted in the beloved Jesus, if you choose to believe it.

Having predestinated us unto the adoption of children by Jesus Christ to Himself, according to the good pleasure of His will, To the praise of the glory of His grace, wherein He has made us accepted in the Beloved."

- Ephesians 1:5-6 (KJV)

Accept that truth. Reject the lie. Love the truth. Hate the lie. If you do well will you not be accepted? Do well by believing the truth that the Father God accepts you in the Beloved Jesus. Once you know that Almighty God accepts you it won't matter to you what foolish man does to you. Man is often foolish and wrong. God is always wise and right. Who are you going to believe? Who ya' gonna' call? If you believe God has made you righteous in the beloved Jesus, then peace and joy will flow out of your heart because you believe God.

Romans 14:17-18 says "the kingdom of God is "righteousness (that state which makes a person acceptable to God) and [heart] peace and joy in the Holy Spirit. He who serves Christ in this way is acceptable and pleasing to God and is approved by men."

You are not a worm; you are a son of the Most High God. Maybe you used to be a wretched worm, but God delivered you and He believes He made you right. I mentioned "Worm theology" in part one; let me explain from scripture what I mean by that.

Romans 7:24-25...
"O unhappy and pitiable and wretched man that I am!"

**(O wretched worm that I am!
Great place to start but dear God don't stop there!)**

"Who will release and deliver me from [the shackles of] this body of death?"

(Great question but please don't stop here either)

"O thank God! [He will!] through Jesus Christ (the Anointed One) our Lord!"

(Now you're getting somewhere!)

"So then indeed I, of myself with the mind and heart, serve the Law of God, but with the flesh the law of sin."

(Now we have some knowledge and understanding so what's the conclusion? What's the bottom line?)

The next verse...

Romans 8:1 says "Therefore, [there is] now no condemnation (no adjudging guilty of wrong) for those who are in Christ Jesus, who live [and] walk not after the dictates of the flesh, but after the dictates of the Spirit."

I got it! I got it! In the spirit I'm always free and in the flesh I'm *always* in bondage. No shame. No guilt, no condemnation in the spirit. Live there. Put your head in the yoke of obedience to Christ and live free indeed! We're not worms. We're saints of the most High God and we have been for 2000 years! What the hell were we thinking? Oh Yeah! We were thinking like hell thinks, but now it's high time to think like heaven! What do you say? God says His thoughts are higher than our thoughts so let's renew our mind to a higher level of thinking so we are more compatible with our Husband Jesus.

Colossians 3:2 says, "And set your minds and keep them set on what is above (the higher things), not on the things that are on the earth."

You are a spirit made in the image of your Creator God. God gave you a mind and a body to use in this physical world and He expects you to use them responsibly just as you might give a car to your teenager and expect them to use it responsibly. However, just like that teenager might not have used his authority to *"just say no,"* so too do we people of God not always use our God given authority as we should. The teenager should have said "no" to booze and sex and we should have said "no" to the devils, to our flesh and to our un-renewed mind.

Let me speak for a moment about authority.

Jesus said in **Luke 10:19** "Behold! I have given you authority and power to trample upon serpents and scorpions, and [physical and mental strength and ability] over all the power that the enemy [possesses]; and nothing shall in any way harm you."

I believe this verse with all my heart and soul but I am impressed to insert a word of balance here. **James 4:7** illustrates my point very well.

> "Submit yourselves therefore to God.
> Resist the devil, and he will flee from you."

> - James 4:7 (ESV)

Question here; does the devil flee because he is afraid of you? Or does he flee because you are subject to Almighty God? What if you are not subject to God? Does the devil still have to flee? What if you have it backwards? What if you resist the things God says but are subject to the things the devil wants you to do? Now does the devil have to flee? I believe your ability to use authority is directly linked to your subjection "to" the authority over you. If you obey, you will be obeyed. Your God given authority will rarely rise above the level to which you are submitted to the authority over you. God's word and His ministers thereof, are the highest authority in the earth. Submit. If you find yourself resisting and rejecting this concept, then you would be wise to examine yourself and see why this concept rubbed you the wrong way.

STEP THREE

Do the unthinkable; accept
responsibility for your freedom.

In releasing sin, guilt and shame the key person is *you*. God gave *you* the keys and said whoever's sins *you* remit are remitted and whoever's sins *you* retain are retained.

And having said this, He breathed on them and said to them, Receive the Holy Spirit! [Now having received the Holy Spirit, and being led and directed by Him] if you forgive the sins of *someone*, they are forgiven; if you retain the sins of *someone*, they are retained.

- John 20:22-23

You're someone. Love the one God loves; you. Now release yourself. Forgive yourself. Pray this: *"Forgive me Father, I have hated the son of God. Myself."* God loves you but you hate you. Somebody has to change their position and God does not change. Pray: *"Forgive me Father God for hating the one You love."* If you can easily say that, you probably don't have a problem with self hatred but if you struggle to say that simple prayer, then your resistance to breathe out this simple prayer may indicate an underlying refusal to love the one that God loves; yourself. Test yourself right now by repeating after me; *"Forgive me Father God for hating the one You love."*

In Part one I read **Romans 9:33** as an encouragement. I want to read it again but this time, view it as more than just encouragement; it's a promise and a way out.

"As it is written, Behold I am laying in Zion a Stone that will make men stumble, a Rock that will make them fall; but he who believes in Him [who adheres to, trusts in, and relies on Him] shall not be PUT TO SHAME nor be disappointed in his expectations."

- Romans 9:33

This is a promise. The closer you get to Jesus the less power shame has over you and yes, the reverse is also true.

"But the path of the [uncompromisingly] just and righteous is like the light of dawn, that shines more and more (brighter and clearer) until [it reaches its full strength and glory in] the perfect day [to be prepared]. The way of the wicked is like deep darkness; they do not know over what they stumble."

- Proverbs 4:18-19

The light that drives out the darkness of shame is the glory that shines in the face of Jesus. Don't turn in shame from His face but rather turn towards Him, even in your shame. You do that by obedience, obedience, obedience. Don't just say the truth, but do the truth. To say the right thing, to say the truth and then not do it is worse than never having known the truth.

In **John 9:41** Jesus said to them, "If you were blind, you would have no sin; "but" because you now claim to have sight, your sin remains. [If you were blind, you would not be guilty of sin; but because you insist, We do see clearly, you are unable to escape your guilt.]"

Hear Truth, do Truth, live Truth.

STEP FOUR

Glory in Christ.

When you're talking about magnets the rule is; opposites attract, but when it comes to spiritual things; opposites repel. I said a moment ago that *"The light that drives out the darkness of shame is the glory that shines in the face of Jesus."* Let me explain what I meant by that. In Part One I briefly touched on the relationship between shame and the glory of God. These are complete opposites and whichever one you focus on will crowd the other completely out of your life if given enough time.

This principle is all over the spiritual realm. Whatever opposites you and I choose to focus on will increase until they completely crowd the opposing and contrary opposite right out of your life. Most Christians try so hard to just stop doing bad things, but I'm sure you've observed by now, that simply does not work. No man can just stop the evil in his life for very long. It always comes back, usually with a vengeance. You know in your heart right now that what I just said is true. Now get this! God does not see the return to evil behavior as a failure on your part. *He knows, that you don't know.* The Father God knows that Jesus asked Him to forgive us because we know not what we do.

God does not want to punish blind men for stepping on peoples toes. *God wants to give blind men sight!* He wants to give stupid people knowledge. He wants to give you and me knowledge so we will have opportunity to replace stupid with smart; replace foolish with wise. Do you see what I'm saying? Stop your vain efforts to resist evil words thoughts and deeds. Just stop it. It has never worked for long because sometime, somewhere evil will flow right back into the empty void you created. We cast out the unclean spirits but Jesus said in **Matthew 12:44** they will soon come back and seven times worse, because the house of your life is EMPTY!

You can't just throw out the unclean spirit and stop there. We must invite the Holy Spirit to clean *and* move into, *and* fill the empty place where the unholy spirit dwelt. Give no place to the devil. Crowd it out by filling your house with the Holy Spirit. Do you see this very important spiritual law yet? Then apply it to your life starting right now while this message is still ringing in your ears.

Romans 12:21 says "Do not let yourself be overcome
by evil, but overcome (master) evil with good."

So I say don't let yourself be overcome by hate, but overcome hate with Love. Don't let yourself be overcome by lies, but overcome lies with Truth, overcome darkness with Light, overcome death with life, overcome wrong with right, overcome pride with humility, rebellion with submission and the list goes on and on but my point in this study is overcome shame with glory. Don't let yourself be overcome by shame, but overcome satan's shame with God's glory. Jesus gave the Fathers glory to you but you were so focused on shame that you gave no place to Glory. You probably don't even realize that God wants to share His glory with you.

> *Well brother Victor; the bible says God*
> *"will not give His glory to another"*

God does say that in **Isaiah 48:11** but if you bother to read the context it's very apparent God was unwilling to share His glory with the pagan, heathen idolatrous enemies of Israel. However the Father is more than willing to share His glory with us, His own children.

Speaking of us, the Bride of Christ, Jesus said in **John 17:22** "I have given to them the glory and honor which You have given Me, that they may be one [even] as We are one."

Be honest with yourself right here; did you even know that verse existed? Did you have any idea that Jesus took the glory that the Father God gave to Him and then Jesus gave it to you and me? Was that concept anywhere in your theology? Why not? I bet you knew we're all sinners didn't you? You knew we all went astray didn't you? You knew there's none righteous no not one, didn't you? So how come we know all the bad stuff about us but we're ignorant of lots of the good stuff?

You'd think there was a lying deceiver running around in the church wouldn't you? You'd think that lying deceiver was trying to put shame on all of us because he wants all the glory for himself but God gave it to us! Lucifer was glorious but he rebelled and was ingloriously thrown down to the earth as lightening. No more glory for him. Then God makes Adam and crowns him with glory. Satan is enraged. He wants his former glory back but God gave it to man by crowning man with glory and honor as **Psalm 8:5** says.

Satan seduces man and tricks us into exchanging our glory for his shame. Jesus comes and once again takes the glory from satan and once again puts shame back on the devil. The devil then sets out to *once again* try to seduce man into exchanging Gods glory for satan's shame but this time *some* of the people of God are not so easily seduced. This time some of the people of God are sticking real close to their Husband the Truth incarnate and they are not buying the shame lie. How close are you?

This time *some* of the virgins are abiding right in the very shadow of their wonderful Husband and they have no intention of trading away the glory their Husband Jesus gave them. Some are drawn away and some keep their eyes fixed on their Jesus whom they love dearly as evidenced by their tendency to cling to His every word as though their life depended on it.

Now do you see how it works? Satan wants to give us his shame and God wants to give us His glory and whichever you choose to cling to, whichever you choose to face, to focus on, in your words and thoughts, will grow and will proportionately crowd the opposite out of your life. Hide your face from all others and trust only your Husband Jesus the Truth to remove your veil.

2 Corinthians 3:16-18 says, "whenever a person turns [in repentance] to the Lord, the veil is stripped off and taken away. Now the Lord is the Spirit, and where the Spirit of the Lord is, there is liberty (emancipation from bondage, freedom). And all of us, as with unveiled face, [because we] continued to behold [in the Word of God] as in a mirror the glory of the Lord, are constantly being transfigured into His very own image in ever increasing splendor and from one degree of glory to another; [for this comes] from the Lord [Who is] the Spirit."

The darkness of shame melts away and the light of God's glory in the face of Jesus consumes the darkness of shame "in ever increasing splendor" and from "one degree of glory to another." Just continue hearing and doing God's word and the word itself contains the power to set you free and keep you free of shame and every other form of dark bondage. And don't say *"I can't"* because God says *"you can do all things through Him"* and if you say "I can't" that means either you or God lied and my God cannot lie. Humility submits to truth but pride seeks after lies to justify its choices. Quit exalting shameful lies over glorious Truth in a vain attempt to justify yourself. God gave you His glory as a gift in Jesus but you keep turning it into shame by seeking after and holding the lie in priority over the Truth.

"O men, how long shall my honor be turned into shame? How long will you love vain words and seek after lies? Selah"

- Psalm 4:2 (ESV)

Selah pause, and calmly think of that! How long? Satan wants you to sin against God because he knows that rebellion will turn your glory into shame and he ought to know because that's exactly what happened to him and his followers.

"You [yourself] will be filled with shame and contempt instead of glory. Drink also and be like an uncircumcised [heathen]! The cup [of wrath] in the Lord's right hand will come around to you [O destroyer], and foul shame shall be upon your own glory!"

- Habakkuk 2:16

"The more they increased and multiplied [in prosperity and power], the more they sinned against Me; I will change their glory into shame."

- Hosea 4:7

Rebellion changes glory into shame and inversely, obedient submission changes shame into glory.

Don't resist truth and don't resist those who bring it to you. Submit. Submit. Submit. Whatever the Truth says, do it. Make a lifestyle of submissive obedience, one scripture at a time. Every day that is called today, do the Truth that day until it becomes your life. Isn't that what you did with lies to get yourself in the mess you're in? You believed lies one day at a time, day in and day out until they became real in your life, didn't you? Simply reverse the process. Live Truth today, and every day that is called today. Start today. Start now. Again I remind you that **John 8:31-32** says that if you live the Truth, you will know the Truth and the truth will make you free. It's a very wise way to live.

"The wise shall inherit glory (all honor and good) but shame is the highest rank conferred on [self-confident] fools."

- Proverbs 3:35

The antidote for shame is the glory all honor and good bestowed upon children of light as they look into the face of Jesus Christ their Lord.

"For God, who said, "Let light shine out of darkness," made his light shine in our hearts to give us the light of the knowledge of the glory of God in the face of Christ."

- 2 Corinthians 4:6 (NIV)

You become like what you focus on. In **Hosea 9:10** God's people turned from the true God and faced the false God of *"that shameful thing [Baal], and they became detestable and loathsome like that which they loved."* I'm going to say it again. The spiritual law, the concept here, and God designed us so, is that whatever you face, or focus your love on, you reflect, like a mirror, until the image is burned into your spirit and you become like the god you choose to face.

> "Beloved, now are we the sons of God, and it doth not yet appear what we shall be: but we know that, when He shall appear, we shall be like Him; for we shall see Him as he is."
>
> - 1 John 3:2 (KJV)

This spiritual law of "becoming like that which we love" shows us the way of escape from shame and fills us with hope for our future.

> Such hope never disappoints or deludes or shames us, for God's love has been poured out in our hearts through the Holy Spirit Who has been given to us.
>
> - Romans 5:5

The Holy Spirit draws us to face Christ and as we do, shame melts away and is replaced by God's glory in the face of Jesus the One Who made it possible for us to come to faith, hope and love. Please don't allow yourself be confused and seduced on this point. The Bible says in four places that shame brings confusion and covers your face so you can't see God and you don't realize what is really going on. In your blinded confusion you may let a stranger into your innermost, intimate heart to dwell where only God should be allowed.

"We are confounded and ashamed, for we have heard reproach; confusion and shame have covered our faces, for strangers have come into the [most] sacred parts of the sanctuary of the Lord."

- Jeremiah 51:51

Reject shame and replace it with the gift of glory by believing what God has said about you. Let me inject a word of balance here. Not all shame is from satan. There is a scriptural place where just cause for shame exists, at least until the moment you repent. In **1st Corinthians 6:5** Paul wrote to Christians, *"I say this to move you to shame"* obviously using shame to move people to a place of positive change. Lazy Christians who won't even open their dusty Bibles may have scriptural cause to be ashamed because:

Study and be eager and do your utmost to present yourself to God approved (tested by trial), *a workman who has no cause to be ashamed,* correctly analyzing and accurately dividing [rightly handling and skillfully teaching] the Word of Truth.

- 2 Timothy 2:15

But if anyone [in the church] refuses to obey what we say in this letter, take note of that person and do not associate with him, so that he may be ashamed.

- 2 Thessalonians 3:14

God can use shame to save the life of even the rebellious. If you believe you may be in rebellion against God listen to these scriptures. *They are your way out of bondage.*

"[As you draw near to God] be deeply penitent and grieve, even weep [over your disloyalty]. Let your laughter be turned to grief and your mirth to dejection and heartfelt shame [for your sins]."

- James 4:9

God loves even the rebels and turns shame into a
good thing to save the rebellious from their destruction.

"Thou hast ascended on high, thou hast led captivity captive: thou hast received gifts for men; yea, for the rebellious also, that the LORD God might dwell among them."

- Psalm 68:18 (KJV)

Listen to **Isaiah 46:8** "[Earnestly] remember this, be ashamed and own yourselves guilty; bring it again to mind and lay it to heart, O you rebels!"

The devil can't make you persist in sin; you can repent any time you want. I've found that people always find a way to do what they really want to do.

As for those who are guilty and PERSIST in sin, rebuke and admonish them in the presence of all, so that the rest may be warned and stand in wholesome awe and fear. I say this to your shame.

- 1 Timothy 5:20

Some are guilty because they persist in sin and like it, but many only think they are still guilty because they simply don't yet realize the cleanness, the rightness that is theirs in Christ because the accuser charges them as wrong day and night until they believe it and he most frequently uses their own thoughts and the ignorant mouth of members of our own household to tear us down and keep us shamed into hiding "alleged" wrongness. Are you forgiven or not? Then live like it. Please don't continue allowing the accuser to use your mouth to blame and condemn yourself, or your own brethren. Let God direct the paths of your thoughts and words.

Listen to the principle of **2 Corinthians 7:10** (NET) "For sadness as intended by God produces a repentance that leads to salvation, leaving no regret, but worldly sadness brings about death."

I believe the principle of allowing God to direct our sadness, or not, also works with shame. If you obey **Proverbs 3:6** and let God direct all your ways then shame could work like this: the shame which God is allowed to direct equals life but the shame which God is not allowed to direct equals death.

"For all who are led by the Spirit of God are sons of God."

- Romans 8:14 (AMP)

The bottom line is; do what you're told. *You can obey, if you will.* When any man resists God that man is actually obeying satan and **Romans 6:16** says you become the slave of whoever you obey. We've been justified but some of us resist Truth and live like the unjust. Be aware that resistance grows into rebellion and a man can sink so deep in rebellion that he sinks beyond shame into spiritual deadness. **Zephaniah 3:5** says the *"unjust [person] knows no shame."* So deep in shame and blinded by pride, that to them evil is good, wrong is right, darkness is light; like they were dead inside.

"But if your eye [your conscience] is unsound, your whole body will be full of darkness. If then the very light in you [your conscience] is darkened, how dense is that darkness!"

- Matthew 6:23

It's like a tomb inside. Caution, don't fall for the self condemnation lie right here. Just the fact that you are even listening to this message full of scripture, is proof you are seeking truth and in God's sight, men who seek truth in their inward parts are justified by their act of seeking God. Never forget that our God can bring life, even to the dead.

STEP FIVE

A clean conscience.

Let me discuss for a moment the concept we call a *guilty conscience*. What exactly is a guilty conscience? For that matter, what is a conscience?

The dictionary defines conscience as:

1. The awareness of a moral or ethical aspect to one's conduct together with the urge to prefer right over wrong, a feeling of obligation to do right or be good.

2. Conformity to one's own sense of right conduct." i.e. "Let your conscience be your guide."

Jesus defines your conscience as
the eye or the lamp of the body.

He says in **Luke 11:34** "Your eye is the lamp of your body; when your eye (your conscience) is sound and fulfilling its office, your whole body is full of light; but when it is not sound and is not fulfilling its office, your body is full of darkness."

That's because the graveclothes of shame cover and encapsulate your spirit. This is the metaphorical mummy I spoke of earlier. In other words, when the eye of your conscience is clean, you see clearly. See what? You see the difference between right and wrong, the difference between truth and lies, between good and evil. But if the eye of your conscience is dirty, as in *"covered with shame,"* these things are all hidden from you as though you were blind, indeed spiritually, you are blind.

Worse still, *you can't clean your own conscience.* No man can escape the condemnation of his own conscience without dying spiritually. No matter how many mighty wonderful religious works we perform; no matter how many gifts and sacrifices we offer up, we still are incapable of removing our own shame, we still can't clean our own conscience. Then what are we to do!?! Glad you asked.

> Let us all come forward and draw near with true (honest and sincere) hearts in unqualified assurance and absolute conviction engendered by FAITH (by that leaning of the entire human personality on God in absolute TRUST and confidence in His power, wisdom, and goodness), having our hearts sprinkled and purified from a guilty (evil) conscience and our bodies cleansed with pure water.
>
> - Hebrews 10:22

Please note that this verse did not say our assurance and confidence before God was derived or engendered by *"our" perfect, flawless performance.*

What does the scripture say? Engendered by FAITH (by that leaning of the entire human personality on God in absolute TRUST and confidence in His power, His wisdom, and His goodness) *Jesus said apart from Him we can do nothing.*

We must come to the conclusion that we are totally dependent upon God and are incapable of cleaning our own conscience. This attitude is called humility and any thought to the contrary, is called pride, which thing God hates. One of the main reasons God hates pride is because He loves us, and He knows that pride destroys us, so God hates that which destroys His child that He loves. We need to learn to love what God loves and to hate what God hates. If a child had cancer the father who loved the child would hate the cancer as he watched it steal, kill and destroy his child. Pride is cancer of the spirit. We should hate what our Father God hates.

> Seeing that that first [outer portion of the] tabernacle was a parable (a visible symbol or type or picture of the present age). In it gifts and sacrifices are offered, and yet are **incapable** of perfecting the conscience or of cleansing and renewing the inner man of the worshiper.
>
> - Hebrews 9:9

So scripture says that all our many mighty wonderful dead works and all our lifeless observances and gifts to God are *"incapable of perfecting the conscience or of cleansing and renewing the inner man."* Yikes! So now what do we do? Again, I'm glad you asked! Our only hope of true change, of real transformation, is by trusting and believing in the power of the Blood of Christ to both clean, and renew our calloused crusted over consciences.

> "How much more surely shall the blood of Christ, Who by virtue of [His] eternal Spirit [His own preexistent divine personality] has offered Himself as an unblemished sacrifice to God, purify our consciences from dead works and lifeless observances to serve the [ever] living God?"
>
> - Hebrews 9:14

Dead works and lifeless observances are religious words and activities about God, but no relationship with God. It is having a form of godliness but no power. Let me read you **2 Timothy 3:4-5** from The Message Bible describing some church folk in the last days:

"treacherous, ruthless, bloated windbags, addicted to lust, and allergic to God. They'll make a show of religion, but behind the scenes they're animals. Stay clear of these people."

We need to immerse ourselves in God, not in religion. That is exactly what our water baptism represents, our immersion in God. Our baptism is a figure, a demonstration, of the truth that just as we disappeared in the baptismal waters and then reemerged a clean new creation, so too are we crucified with Christ then raised with Him to a new life.

"And baptism, which is a figure [of their deliverance], does now also save you [from inward questionings and fears], **not** by the removing of outward body filth [bathing], but by [providing you with] the answer of a good and clear **conscience** (inward cleanness and peace) before God [because **you are demonstrating what you believe** to be yours] through the resurrection of Jesus Christ."

- 1 Peter 3:21

I said in part one of this message I'd come back to **1st John 3:20-21** because it's very important that we understand this concept *if we are to be free of shame.* In the Amplified Bible it reads like this;

"**Whenever** our hearts in [tormenting] **self-accusation** make us feel guilty and condemn us. [For we are in God's hands.] He is above and greater than our consciences (our hearts), and He knows (perceives and understands) everything [nothing is hidden from Him]. :21 And, beloved, if our consciences (our hearts) do not accuse us [if they do not make us feel guilty and condemn us], we have **confidence** (complete assurance and boldness) before God."

- 1 John 3:20-21

In other words, at the new birth, God cleaned and renewed our dirty, darkness and relit the lamp of our conscience. That's why Paul who was doing shameful things to Christians in **Acts 8:3** and **9:1** can say in **Acts 23:1** *"Brethren, I have lived before God, doing my duty with a perfectly good conscience until this very day."*

Say what? How can he say that after what he'd done? He can say it by faith because he believed God and it was credited to his account as rightness before God, the final Judge of all mankind. Paul believed God more than he believed his own shame, guilt and condemnation and we should grow up in faith and learn to do likewise.

"Therefore if any person is [ingrafted] in Christ (the Messiah) he is a new creation (a new creature altogether); the old [previous moral and spiritual condition] has passed away. Behold, the fresh and new has come!"

- 2 Corinthians 5:17

Do you believe that? If you really do, then you have nothing to be ashamed of, no matter what you know you did. Now that's shame free! But you might say, *"It can't be that easy."* To which I would reply, *"Quit pridefully leaning to your own understanding and humble yourself before Almighty God."*

You are what He says you are, if you believe it. Do you believe it? Then you are shame free. If you don't believe then you remain a prisoner of shame because you choose unbelief over believing the word of almighty God. It's your choice and it always has been. This is the secret of the Christian faith and it is only revealed to those who "say," I believe you God! Those who choose to stay in unbelief, continue in their bondage as though they were ungodly men, and the secret of freedom by faith is hidden from them until they repent of their unbelief.

"They must possess the mystic secret of the faith [Christian truth as hidden from ungodly men] with a clear conscience."

- 1 Timothy 3:9

Jesus already solved our shame problem. You need only believe the truth Jesus speaks, more than and rather than the lies that shame whispers to you. Repent right now. Just pause and tell God sorry.

If you couldn't bring yourself to repent of unbelief just now it's probably because your shame and unbelief are hardened into place by pride. My Godly wife said that pride is the glue that holds shame in place and hardens the grave clothes into a tough impervious shell, like a coffin. I searched the scriptures and sure enough *the Bible shows a clear connection between pride & shame.*

"When swelling and pride come, then emptiness and shame come also, but with the humble (those who are lowly, who have been pruned or chiseled by trial, and renounce self) are skillful and godly Wisdom and soundness."

- Proverbs 11:2

I would instruct you to cry out to God for humility
while you still can or you risk losing everything.

"Poverty and shame come to him who refuses instruction and correction, but he who heeds reproof is honored."

- Proverbs 13:18

For both He Who sanctifies [making men holy] and those who are sanctified all have one [Father]. For this reason He is not ashamed to call them brethren;

- Hebrews 2:11

Hebrews 11:16 shows that because the people "were yearning for and aspiring to a better and more desirable place, that is, a heavenly [one]. For that reason God is not ashamed to be called their God."

The very attitude that causes you to seek to be better is enough to cause Almighty God to not be ashamed to be called your God. Do you desire to be more Christlike? Then God is not ashamed of you so why should you be ashamed of you? Unless of course, you know more than God, in which case, you better read some more scripture on pride.

I ended Part One of this study talking about Trust and I want to close Part Two with this same indispensable concept of trusting God.

"I assure you, most solemnly I tell you, the person whose ears are open to My words [who listens to My message] and believes and **TRUSTS** in and clings to and relies on Him Who sent Me has (possesses now) eternal life. And he does not come into judgment [does not incur sentence of judgment, will not come under condemnation], but he has already passed over out of death into life."

- John 5:24

(But you have to open your ears and
listen to the message. Are you listening?)

The Scripture says, "No man who believes in Him [who adheres to, relies on, and **TRUSTS** in Him] will [ever] be put to shame or be disappointed."

- Romans 10:11

"...he who believes (**TRUSTS** in, relies on, and adheres to that Stone, (Jesus) will not be ashamed."

- Isaiah 28:16

"And you shall know, understand, and realize that I am in the midst of you (that's the 2 or 3 gathered together in Matthew 18:20) and that I the Lord am your God and *My people shall never be put to shame.*"

- Joel 2:27

"...let me not be ashamed or disappointed, for my **TRUST** and my refuge are in You."

- Psalm 25:20

I have to sound a warning here. None of us have any promise that we can take as long as we please before we "do God a big favor" by finally choosing to trust Him. God always gives space to repent but the God I know won't strive with man forever. Just as with any other bondage or deception, when someone has had space to repent but still refuses the Shepherds call to come out of severe shame bondage, there will come a time when God will let you go and He will instruct His ministers to let you go. Jesus taught in the parable of the prodigal son that there is a time to let them go and just as the father in the prodigal story let the son go completely, not partially, so also will we have to be willing to let go and let God. If we can't let go it's because we either don't trust God or we trust ourselves more than God, or both.

Ecclesiastes 3:5-6 says there is "A time to cast away stones and a time to gather stones together, ...

(God says we are lively stones, fitly joined together)

...a time to embrace and a time to refrain from embracing, 6 A time to get and a time to lose, a time to keep and a time to cast away,"

Also, **1st Peter 5:7** Says we humble ourselves by casting all our care onto Him and inversely, if we cannot commit the care of our self, or someone else fully over to God, it's pride. Simply put, I trust me, more than I trust God. Repent. Trust God.

If He says to let them go, then let them go. God has done this and it works. I have done this at His command, and it works. You can do this when He tells you to but there is a spiritual principle here which makes letting them go much easier. When the time comes that you have to let someone go because they refuse to listen and repent, please don't close the book on them, just close the current chapter, looking forward with joy to the hopeful expectation that God will set before them that trust Him. This is not the end of their story. It's just the end of the current chapter. Jesus did this at the cross.

"Looking unto Jesus the author and finisher of our faith; who *for the joy that was set before Him* endured the cross, despising the shame, and is set down at the right hand of the throne of God."

- Hebrews 12:2

Shame is your enemy; treat it as such.

"Unto thee, O LORD, do I lift up my soul. :2 O my God, I **trust** in Thee: let me not be ashamed, let not mine enemies triumph over me."

- Psalm 25:1-2

Shame is your enemy. Cry out to God, *"Let not my enemy triumph over me."* Be dependent on God. Trust in, rely on and cling to God. I usually close in prayer, but with this message I'm led to let my closing prayer for you be the words of this anointed song based on **Psalm 25.** I believe this song will ring in your spirit and the words echo in your soul long after you have finished this message.

Unto Thee O Lord

From Psalm 25

The audio for this song is at the end of the
audio book for part two, available here:

1. Unto Thee O Lord, Do I lift up my soul. (2x)

(Chorus)
Oh my God, I trust in Thee,
Let me not be ashamed,
let not my enemies triumph over me.

2. Let none that wait, on Thee be ashamed. (2x)

3. Show me Thy ways, Lord teach me Thy paths. (2x)

4. Call me out O Lord, take my grave clothes away. (2x)

5. Where else would I go, You have the words of Life. (2x)

6. I love You Lord, because You first loved me. (2x)

7. Lead me in thy truth, on thee do I wait. (2x)

8. Remember not my sin, show thy mercy for me. (2x)

9. Good and upright are You, so You taught me Your ways. (2x)

10. All the paths of the LORD, are mercy and truth. (2x)

11. The secret of the LORD, is with them that fear Him. (2x)

12. I am hid in Christ; I dwell in Your secret place. (2x)

More Teachings

In addition to this book, there are many additional teachings from Victor Chatellier you can listen to for free at:

thevoiceoftruth.net

or simply scan the QR Code below.

ABOUT THE AUTHOR

By himself Victor is really and truly a nobody. But Victor is not by himself, he is with Jesus, and they talk, *a lot*. This book is the fruit of those conversations. Taste and see.

"When they saw the boldness of Peter and John, and discovered that they were uneducated and ordinary men, they were amazed and recognized these men had been with Jesus"

- Acts 4:13 (NET)

<u>Notes</u>

Made in United States
Troutdale, OR
12/23/2024